June 2012

MANAGING FOR RESULTS

A Guide for Using the GPRA Modernization Act to Help Inform Congressional Decision Making

Contents

Abbreviations

2008 Leadership Act	Tom Lantos and Henry J. Hyde United States Global Leadership Against HIV/AIDS, Tuberculosis, and Malaria Reauthorization Act of 2008
DHS	Department of Homeland Security
GPRA	Government Performance and Results Act of 1993
GPRAMA	GPRA Modernization Act of 2010
IPERA	Improper Payments Elimination and Recovery Act of 2010
IPIA	Improper Payments Information Act of 2002
OGAC	Office of the U.S. Global AIDS Coordinator
OIG	Office of Inspector General
OMB	Office of Management and Budget
PEPFAR	President's Emergency Plan for AIDS Relief
USCIS	United States Citizenship and Immigration Services

United States Government Accountability Office
Washington, DC 20548

June 15, 2012

The Honorable Daniel K. Akaka
Chairman
Subcommittee on Oversight of Government Management, the Federal
  Workforce, and the District of Columbia
Committee on Homeland Security and Governmental Affairs
United States Senate

The Honorable Thomas R. Carper
Chairman
Subcommittee on Federal Financial Management, Government
  Information, Federal Services, and International Security
Committee on Homeland Security and Governmental Affairs
United States Senate

The Honorable Mark R. Warner
Chairman
Task Force on Government Performance
Committee on the Budget
United States Senate

Many of the meaningful results that the federal government seeks to
achieve, such as those related to protecting food and agriculture,
providing homeland security, and ensuring a well-trained and educated
workforce, require the coordinated efforts of more than one federal
agency. As Congress creates, modifies, and funds federal programs and
activities, it needs pertinent and reliable information to adequately assess
agencies' progress in meeting established performance goals, ensure
accountability for results, and understand how individual programs and
activities fit within a broader portfolio of federal efforts.

However, as our annual reports on duplication, overlap, and
fragmentation in the federal government have recently highlighted, there
are a number of crosscutting areas where performance information is

limited or does not exist.[1] Even in instances where agencies produce a great deal of performance information, our past work has shown that it does not always reach the interested parties in Congress, and when it does, the information may not be timely or presented in a manner that is useful for congressional decision making.[2]

To help ensure that executive branch performance information is useful to Congress for its decision making, congressional involvement on what to measure and how to present this information is critical. Recognizing this, Congress updated the statutory framework for performance management in the federal government, the Government Performance and Results Act of 1993 (GPRA), with the GPRA Modernization Act of 2010 (GPRAMA),[3] which significantly enhances the requirements for agencies to consult with Congress when establishing or adjusting governmentwide and agency goals. Specifically, the Office of Management and Budget (OMB) is required to consult with relevant committees with broad jurisdiction on crosscutting priority goals.[4] Agencies are to consult with their relevant appropriations, authorization, and oversight committees when developing or making adjustments to their strategic plans and agency priority goals.

This guide, prepared at your request, is intended to assist Members of Congress and their staffs in (1) ensuring the consultations required under GPRAMA are useful to the Congress and (2) using performance information produced by executive branch agencies in carrying out various congressional decision-making responsibilities, such as

---

[1]GAO, *2012 Annual Report: Opportunities to Reduce Duplication, Overlap and Fragmentation, Achieve Savings, and Enhance Revenue*, GAO-12-342SP (Washington, D.C.: Feb. 28, 2012), and *Opportunities to Reduce Potential Duplication in Government Programs, Save Tax Dollars, and Enhance Revenue*, GAO-11-318SP (Washington, D.C.: Mar. 1, 2011).

[2]GAO, *Congressional Oversight: FAA Case Study Shows How Agency Performance, Budgeting, and Financial Information Could Enhance Oversight*, GAO-06-378, (Washington, D.C.: Mar. 8, 2006).

[3]Pub. L. No. 111-352, 124 Stat. 3866 (2011). GPRAMA amends GPRA, Pub. L. No. 103-62, 107 Stat. 285 (1993).

[4]OMB is required to consult with the Senate and House Committees on Appropriations, the Senate and House Committees on the Budget, the Senate Committee on Homeland Security and Governmental Affairs, the House Committee on Oversight and Government Reform, the Senate Committee on Finance, the House Committee on Ways and Means, and any other committees as determined appropriate. 31 U.S.C. § 1120(a)(3).

authorizing programs or provisions in the tax code, making appropriations, developing budgets, and providing oversight.

To develop the guide, we reviewed consultation requirements specified in the act, as well as the related intent, and identified general approaches for successful consultations by reviewing our prior reports, observing a recent consultation between agency officials and congressional committee staff, and interviewing officials from several selected agencies about their past consultation experiences. To illustrate how Congress can use performance information, we selected three case studies from our prior work in which Congress played an active role in contributing to and overseeing agency efforts to improve performance. The case studies cover federal efforts to

- transform the processing of immigration benefits;
- coordinate U.S. efforts to address the global HIV/AIDS pandemic; and
- identify and address improper payments made by federal programs.

In addition, we recently provided briefings to various congressional staff on several other case studies.[5] In compiling these examples, we reviewed legislation, related congressional documents, our related past work, as well as that conducted by agency inspectors general.

We conducted our work from December 2010 to June 2012 in accordance with all sections of GAO's Quality Assurance Framework that are relevant to our objectives. The framework requires that we plan and perform the engagement to obtain sufficient and appropriate evidence to meet our stated objectives and to discuss any limitations in our work. We believe that the information and data obtained, and the analysis conducted, provide a reasonable basis for any findings and conclusions in this product.

---

[5]See GAO, *Managing for Results: Opportunities for Congress to Address Government Performance Issues*, GAO-12-215R (Washington, D.C.: Dec. 9, 2011). The case studies contained in the briefing covered efforts to consolidate four overlapping bilingual education programs, reform the personnel security clearance process to reduce backlogs, and shift from paper to electronic filing of tax returns.

We are sending copies of this guide to interested congressional committees and the Director of OMB. In addition, the guide is available at no charge on the GAO website at http://www.gao.gov.

If you or your staff have any questions about this guide, please contact me at (202) 512-6806 or mihmj@gao.gov. Contact points for our Offices of Congressional Relations and Public Affairs may be found on the last page of this report. GAO staff who made key contributions to this guide are listed in appendix II.

J. Christopher Mihm
Managing Director, Strategic Issues

Introduction to the Guide

Performance information can cover a range of related topics, including the results the federal government should seek to achieve, how those results will be achieved, how progress will be measured, and how results will be reported.[1] To ensure that their performance information will be both useful and used by decision makers, agencies need to consider the differing information needs of various users—including those in Congress. As we have previously reported, agency performance information must meet Congress's needs for completeness, accuracy, validity, timeliness, and ease of use to be useful for congressional decision making.[2] As noted in our past work, several requirements put into place by GPRAMA could help address those needs.[3]

- *Completeness:* Agencies often lack information on the effectiveness of programs; such information could help decision makers prioritize resources among programs. Our work on overlap and duplication has found crosscutting areas where performance information is limited or does not exist. The crosscutting planning and reporting requirements could lead to the development of performance information in areas that are currently incomplete.
- *Accuracy and validity:* Agencies are required to disclose more information about the accuracy and validity of their performance information in their performance plans and reports, including the sources for their data and actions to address limitations to the data.
- *Timeliness and ease of use:* Quarterly reporting for cross-agency and agency priority goals, along with posting much of the governmentwide and agency performance information on a central, governmentwide website, will provide more timely, accessible, and easy-to-use information.

How to Use This Guide

Section I describes how Members of Congress and their staffs can influence the development of performance information that meets congressional needs through consultations with executive branch

---

[1]For more information about the performance information required under the federal performance management framework, see GAO-12-215R, 30-51.

[2]GAO, *Managing for Results: Enhancing Agency Use of Performance Information for Management Decision Making*, GAO-05-927 (Washington, D.C.: Sept. 9, 2005).

[3]GAO, *Managing for Results: GPRA Modernization Act Implementation Provides Important Opportunities to Address Government Challenges*, GAO-11-617T (Washington, D.C.: May 10, 2011).

agencies. This section identifies the requirements for these consultations, as well as the related congressional intent. In appendix I, the guide presents key questions that Members and congressional staff can ask as part of the consultation to ensure that agency performance information reflects congressional priorities. Finally, this section provides general approaches for ensuring consultations are successful.

Section II illustrates how Congress can use performance information in its various legislative and oversight decision making activities to identify issues to address, measure the federal government's progress towards addressing those issues, and when necessary, identify better strategies to address those issues. In this section, three case studies demonstrate how Congress has used performance information to inform its decision making in these different ways.

How We Developed This Guide

This guide builds upon a large body of work we have conducted during the past two decades related to performance management in the federal government. This includes a number of products focused on enhancing the usefulness and use of performance information in congressional decision making,[4] including our recent briefings to congressional staff on opportunities for Congress to address government performance issues.[5]

To identify how Congress can use the consultations required under GPRAMA, we identified requirements specified in the act, as well as the intent of these requirements as reported by the Senate Committee on Homeland Security and Governmental Affairs.[6] Additionally, we identified illustrative questions Congress can ask during consultations and general approaches for successful consultations by reviewing our prior reports. We determined whether the approaches identified in a past report have remained relevant through several means.[7] This included observing—at the invitation of congressional committee staff—a recent consultation with

---

[4]See "Related GAO Products" at the end of this guide for a list.

[5]GAO-12-215R.

[6]S. Rep. No. 111-372 (2010).

[7]GAO, *Managing for Results, Enhancing the Usefulness of GPRA Consultations Between the Executive Branch and Congress*, GAO/T-GGD-97-56 (Washington, D.C.: Mar. 10, 1997).

agency officials, and interviewing performance improvement and legislative affairs officials from several selected agencies about their past consultation experiences.[8] We also gathered the views of current and former congressional and agency staff who participated in a forum held on July 5, 2011, by the National Academy of Public Administration on structuring collaboration between Congress and the executive branch on reporting, receiving, and using performance information.[9] Our samples are nongeneralizeable given the methods used to select the congressional staff and agency officials involved in the consultation, interviews, and forum.

To illustrate how Congress can use performance information produced by agencies to carry out its responsibilities, we selected three case studies from our prior work in which Congress played an active role in contributing to and overseeing agency efforts to improve performance. The case studies cover federal efforts to

- transform the processing of immigration benefits;
- coordinate U.S. efforts to address the global HIV/AIDS pandemic; and
- identify and address improper payments made by federal programs.

In compiling these examples, we reviewed legislation, related congressional documents, and our related past work as well as that conducted by agency inspectors general. The case studies are based on publicly available information and are not intended to represent a complete list of all legislative and oversight activities conducted by Congress, but rather illustrate the types of activities that Congress has engaged in when using performance information. Although they focus on congressional activities, the progress and results achieved in these

---

[8]We interviewed officials from the Department of the Interior, Department of the Treasury, Small Business Administration, and Social Security Administration. An OMB official recommended these agencies and officials to us based on their involvement in Performance Improvement Council working groups focused on implementing GPRAMA and the useful past experiences with congressional consultations they shared during those working group sessions.

[9]Nine current and former congressional staff members participated in the forum. This bipartisan, bicameral group of staff worked for appropriations, budget, and governmentwide oversight committees and subcommittees. Current and former executive branch officials from OMB, the Office of Personnel Management, Department of the Interior, Department of State, National Aeronautics and Space Administration, and Social Security Administration shared their views during the forum.

examples are due in part to the sustained attention and oversight of both the executive branch and Congress.

We conducted our work from December 2010 to June 2012 in accordance with all sections of GAO's Quality Assurance Framework that are relevant to our objectives. The framework requires that we plan and perform the engagement to obtain sufficient and appropriate evidence to meet our stated objectives and to discuss any limitations in our work. We believe that the information and data obtained, and the analysis conducted, provide a reasonable basis for any findings and conclusions in this product.

Section I: Consultations Provide Congress with Opportunities to Influence Development of Executive Branch Performance Information That Is Useful for Decision Making

Consultations Are Intended to Strengthen Collaboration between the Congress and Federal Agencies

GPRAMA requires OMB and agencies to consult with relevant committees, obtaining majority and minority views, about proposed goals at least once every 2 years. Specifically, OMB is required to consult with relevant committees with broad jurisdiction on crosscutting priority goals.[1] Agencies are to consult with their relevant appropriations, authorization, and oversight committees when developing or making adjustments to their strategic plans and agency priority goals. The act also requires OMB, on a governmentwide website, and agencies, in their strategic plans, to describe how input provided during consultations was incorporated into the crosscutting priority goals and agency goals, respectively.

According to the Senate report accompanying the act, consultations are intended to strengthen collaboration between Congress and federal agencies to improve government performance.[2] Successful strategic planning requires the involvement of key stakeholders, which can help build consensus. We have long noted the importance of the executive branch considering Congress a partner in shaping goals at the outset. As the committee report notes, the consultation process was established so agencies could take congressional views into account as appropriate. If an agency waits to consult with relevant congressional stakeholders until a strategic plan has been substantially drafted and fully vetted within the executive branch, it foregoes important opportunities to learn about and address early on specific concerns that will be critical to successful implementation. The committee, therefore, emphasized that consultations should take place during the development of a strategic plan, not after. In addition, the requirement for consultations at least once every 2 years is intended to ensure that each Congress has input on agency goals, objectives, strategies, and performance measures. Consultations also provide agencies with opportunities to share information on their

---

[1] OMB is required to consult with the Senate and House Committees on Appropriations, the Senate and House Committees on the Budget, the Senate Committee on Homeland Security and Governmental Affairs, the House Committee on Oversight and Government Reform, the Senate Committee on Finance, the House Committee on Ways and Means, and any other committees as determined appropriate.

[2] S. Rep. No. 111-372, at 4 (2010).

performance and confirm that various committees are getting the types of performance information they need.

In appendix I, we provide an illustrative list of questions that Members of Congress and their staffs can use during consultations to help ensure they provide input on key aspects of an agency's performance information.

Creating Shared Expectations and Engaging the Right People at the Right Time Can Help Ensure Consultations Are Successful

Consultations provide an important opportunity for Congress and the executive branch to work together to ensure that agency missions are focused, goals are specific and results-oriented, and strategies and funding expectations are appropriate and reasonable. Willingness on the part of Congress and the administration to work together is a likely precondition to successful consultations. Discussions between the executive and legislative branches about performance are likely to underscore the competing and conflicting goals of many federal programs, as well as sometimes differing expectations between the branches. In addition, the historical relationships between an agency and Congress, the strategic issues facing the agency, and the degree of policy agreement or disagreement within Congress and between Congress and the administration on those issues will influence the way consultations are carried out. Although constructive communication across the branches of government can prove difficult, it is essential for sustaining federal performance improvement efforts.

Create Shared Expectations

Tailor Consultations and Information Provided to Meet Participants' Needs

In our prior work as well as the work done for this guide, both committee staff and agency officials stressed that agencies should tailor their consultations based on the experiences and needs of those involved. However, they often presented differing views on the desired level of detail for consultations. Congressional staff, on the whole, wanted a deeper examination of the agency's strategic plan and overall performance. These views reflect part of Congress's intent in requiring these consultations—that they provide each Congress with an opportunity to provide input on not only the agency's goals and objectives, but also its strategies, performance measures, and presentation of performance information. Some agency officials agreed, observing that agencies should be prepared to have broader discussions about their performance—beyond what is in the plans. Other agency officials, however, shared a view that consultations were to focus on strategic plans, not issues related to specific programs. As a result, these agency officials said they wanted discussions kept at a higher level—for example, on the agency's mission and strategic goals. While neither of these views is necessarily right or wrong, these expressed differences highlight the need to create shared expectations about what will be covered during consultation sessions.

Committee staff also told us that they encouraged agencies to provide them with relevant documents, including drafts of strategic plans, before the meetings. This enabled them to prepare questions and suggestions in advance. It also helped them focus on presentations and discussions taking place during the meetings by eliminating the need to read and respond to the documents at the same time. Another committee staff member stressed the importance of limiting the materials provided to those most critical, because congressional staff workloads constrain the time available to read such documents. Agency officials we spoke with echoed these views and stated that they provided congressional staff with draft materials in advance. For example, an official from one agency told us that he provided the agency's strategic plan framework—its mission and goals—in lieu of the entire draft plan, which helped focus the consultation on overarching policy issues and the agency's long-term goals.

Promote a Mutual Understanding of Priorities

Successful consultations can create a basic understanding among stakeholders of the competing demands that confront most agencies and congressional staff, the limited resources available to them, and how those demands and resources require careful and continuous balancing. The requirement under GPRAMA for agencies to consult with Congress on the identification of priority goals presents an opportunity to develop such an understanding, especially given Congress's constitutional role in setting national priorities and allocating the resources to achieve them. Several agency officials told us that feedback provided by Members and congressional staff on their agencies' overarching goals and strategies helped them understand congressional priorities.

Engage the Right People at the Right Time

Be Open to an Iterative Process, Engaging Congress at the Appropriate Times

The committee staff and agency officials we spoke with acknowledged that the consultation process was iterative. All agreed that they should meet as many times as both sides feel is necessary. Agency officials told us that consultations were most useful if they began early, during the drafting of the strategic plan. Congress also emphasized this point in the report accompanying GPRAMA. One agency official stated that getting congressional input at the beginning of the process gave the agency time to reconcile any differences in opinion on the agency's direction. Agency officials also cautioned against waiting too long to consult with Congress. Officials from two agencies shared similar past experiences in which they provided a full draft strategic plan for congressional review, which was the extent of their consultation process. In both cases, the agencies received little or no feedback. As a result, both now consult earlier in the process. However, officials told us it was still important to share the draft plan for comment later in the process.

Begin Consultations at the Staff Level

Congressional staff and agency officials agreed that consultations should begin at the staff level—that is, without Members of Congress and agency top leadership—and involve agency officials with varying responsibilities. Both congressional committee staff and agency officials stressed the importance of having agency officials who can answer specific program-related questions attend, as well as those with authority to revise the agency's plans. Examples include the performance improvement officer, staff from policy and program areas, and representatives from the legislative affairs office. According to committee staff members, the involvement of program officials is more likely to ensure that consultations are informative for both Congress and the agency.

Over Time, Involve Members of Congress and Agency Top Leadership as Appropriate

As the consultations proceed, the involvement of Members of Congress and agency leadership is important because they are ultimately responsible for making decisions about the agency's strategic direction and funding. Officials from one agency told us that they thought the involvement of their top leaders in consultations with Members of Congress and their staff has helped their agency receive attention from Congress. For example, they shared that it has helped raise awareness and a better understanding in Congress of the challenges the agency faces. In addition to participating in consultations, congressional staff suggested several ways in which Members could be involved in agency performance management efforts. For example, Members could send letters to agencies posing questions on strategic plans and formally documenting their views on key issues. Another staff member said that hearings are important because not only do they result in Member involvement, but they also require the participation of senior agency leaders. Holding hearings following consultation sessions can create a public record of agreements reached during those sessions and provide oversight on agency performance planning efforts.

To the Extent Practicable, Conduct Bipartisan Consultations and Coordinate across Committees and Chambers

Congressional staff and agency officials generally agreed that consultations ideally should be bipartisan and bicameral to help ensure involvement from all relevant parties. Although it may not always be possible, agency officials told us that they attempted to arrange such sessions, as appropriate. When these agencies were successful in doing so—as was the case with two agencies, according to officials with whom we spoke—it was with majority and minority staff from corresponding committees across the chambers (e.g., appropriations subcommittees).

In addition, to the extent feasible, consultations should be held jointly with relevant authorizing, appropriations, budget, and oversight committees. Committee staff recognized that, due to sometimes overlapping jurisdictions, obtaining the involvement of all interested congressional committees in a coordinated approach can be challenging. However, the often overlapping or fragmented nature of federal programs—a problem that has been extensively documented in our work—underscores the importance of a coordinated consultation process. For example, in an attempt to address this issue during initial implementation of GPRA in 1997, the House leadership formed teams of congressional staff from different committees to have a direct role in the consultation process.

Section II: Case Studies Illustrate How Congress Uses Performance Information to Inform Its Decision Making

Performance information can be used to inform congressional decisions about authorizing or reauthorizing federal programs, provisions in the tax code, and other activities; appropriating funds; and developing budget resolutions. In this section, three case studies demonstrate how Congress has used performance information to inform its decision making

1. to identify issues that the federal government should address;
2. to measure the federal government's progress toward addressing those issues; and
3. when necessary, to identify better strategies to address the issues.

The case studies cover efforts to

- transform the processing of immigration benefits;
- coordinate U.S. efforts to address the global HIV/AIDS pandemic; and
- identify and address improper payments made by federal programs.

These case studies—as well as those included in our recent briefings[1]—also demonstrate how Congress can assist agencies in developing and achieving performance goals. For example, in many of these examples, Congress set clear expectations for agency performance, required routine reporting on progress, and provided consistent oversight over a sustained period of time. When an agency fell short of meeting established goals, Congress examined whether additional authority would help the agency meet the goal and, when needed, provided such authority. In one case study, Congress required an agency to develop and submit a strategic plan prior to receiving a portion of its appropriations.

Performance Information Can Help Congress Identify Issues to Address

Members of Congress, congressional committees and staff can use performance information about the outcomes of federal programs to identify pressing issues for the federal government to address. The transformation of the United States Citizenship and Immigration Services's (USCIS) benefits processing illustrates how information on an agency's performance helped Congress identify issues to address and act upon.

---

[1]GAO-12-215. The case studies contained in the briefings covered efforts to consolidate four overlapping bilingual education programs, reform the personnel security clearance process to reduce backlogs, and shift from paper to electronic filing of tax returns.

Case Illustration:
Transforming USCIS's
Processing of Benefits

USCIS, a component of the Department of Homeland Security (DHS), adjudicates benefits requests and petitions for individuals seeking to become citizens of the United States or to study, live, or work in this country. Our past work, and that of the DHS Office of Inspector General (OIG), has identified performance challenges USCIS faces in processing benefits. For example, a 2005 DHS OIG report found that USCIS's ability to annually process more than 7 million benefit applications has been hindered by inefficient, paper-based processes, resulting in a backlog that peaked in 2004 at more than 3.8 million cases.[2] Recognizing that dependence on paper files makes it difficult to process immigration benefits efficiently, USCIS began a transformation initiative in 2005 to transition to electronic processing to enhance customer service, improve efficiency, and prevent future backlogs of immigration benefit applications.

Recognizing the importance of this transformation initiative, Congress provided USCIS with $181,990,000 in appropriations in fiscal year 2007,[3] which included, according to the Conference Committee report, $47 million to upgrade its information technology and business systems.[4] However, before USCIS could obligate this funding, Congress directed the agency to submit a strategic transformation plan and expenditure plan with details on expected performance and deliverables. Congress also directed us to review and report to the appropriations committees on the plans. According to a House Committee on Appropriations report that accompanied the act, the committee wanted to ensure that USCIS's transformation efforts were consistent with best practices.[5] In May 2007, USCIS submitted its Transformation Program Strategic Plan and Expenditure Plan to the appropriations committees. We briefed the committees in June and July 2007 on our review, which found that USCIS's plans had mixed success in addressing key practices for organizational transformations. As illustrated in table 1, more than half of the key practices (five out of nine) were either partially or not addressed.

---

[2]Department of Homeland Security, Office of Inspector General, *USCIS Faces Challenges in Modernizing Information Technology*, OIG-05-41 (Washington, D.C.: September 2005).

[3]Department of Homeland Security Appropriations Act, 2007, Pub. L. No. 109-295, 120 Stat. 1355, 1374 (2006).

[4]H. Rep. No. 109-699, at 165 (2006).

[5]H. Rep. No. 109-476, at 105 (2006).

Our report noted that more attention was needed in a number of management-related activities, including performance measurement.[6]

---

[6]GAO, *USCIS Transformation: Improvements to Performance, Human Capital, and Information Technology Management Needed as Modernization Proceeds*, GAO-07-1013R (Washington, D.C.: July 17, 2007).

Table 1: GAO's Assessment of USCIS's 2007 Transformation Program Strategic Plan's Conformance with Key Practices

Key practice	Fully addressed	Partially addressed	Not addressed	Summary of findings
1. Ensure top leadership drives the transformation.	X			USCIS took several actions to ensure top leadership drove the transformation, such as establishing a Transformation Program Office that directly reports to the USCIS Deputy Director.
2. Establish a coherent mission and integrated strategic goals to guide the transformation.	X			USCIS established a mission, vision, and strategic goals in its Strategic Plan that could have been used to guide the transformation.
3. Focus on a key set of principles and priorities at the outset of the transformation.	X			USCIS identified priorities and a succinct set of core values with which to guide the transformation and help build a new agencywide culture.
4. Set implementation goals and a timeline to build momentum and show progress from day one.		X		USCIS established high-level implementation goals and a timeline for the transformation, but had not shared them with all employees and stakeholders, a step that would have helped build momentum and illustrate progress.
5. Dedicate an implementation team to manage the transformation process and involve key stakeholders.		X		USCIS dedicated an implementation team to manage the transformation and involved stakeholders on an as-needed basis; however, its Federal Stakeholder Advisory Board had not yet convened.
6. Use the performance management system to define responsibility and assure accountability for change.			X	USCIS was not using its performance management system to define expectations and hold employees accountable for the transformation.
7. Establish a communication strategy to create shared expectations and report related progress.		X		USCIS completed an initial communication strategy and began exchanging information with employees and stakeholders. However, the strategy for 2008 and beyond was not clearly defined, and lacked an effective approach for communicating with stakeholders.
8. Involve employees to obtain their ideas and gain ownership for the transformation.	X			USCIS took several steps to involve employees in the transformation, and was planning for additional involvement as the transformation progressed.
9. Build a world-class organization using leading practices in strategic human capital management, performance measurement, and information technology management.		X		USCIS was conducting benchmarking research to identify leading business processes, but its plans did not adequately consider information technology management controls, strategic human capital management, and performance measurement to build a world-class organization.

Source: GAO-07-1013R.

Since then, Congress has continued to provide oversight on, and raise concerns about the performance of, USCIS's transformation initiative, which is ongoing. For example, several committees held at least six hearings related to USCIS's transformation plan from 2007 to 2011, including appropriations hearings in 2008 and 2010 during which committee members expressed concerns about USCIS not meeting its goals for timely processing of applications and implementing its transformation plan. In February 2011, the Ranking Member of the Senate Committee on the Judiciary—which has jurisdiction over immigration issues—wrote a letter to the Director of USCIS expressing concern over reported delays and cost increases for completing the transformation and requested a briefing on the effort. In addition, in response to congressional requests, we have reviewed aspects of USCIS's implementation of its transformation plan. For example, in September 2011 we reported that while USCIS had improved the quality and efficiency of the immigration benefit administration process and strengthened its immigration fraud detection and deterrence efforts, the agency's efforts to modernize its benefit processing infrastructure and business practices missed planned milestones by more than two years.[7] In November 2011, we reported that a lack of defined requirements, an acquisition strategy, and associated cost parameters contributed to the delays and noted that consistent adherence to DHS's acquisition policy could help improve USCIS' transformation program outcomes.[8] In particular, we reported that USCIS was managing the program without specific acquisition management controls, such as reliable schedules, which detail work to be performed by both the government and its contractor over the expected life of the program. As a result, we found that USCIS does not have reasonable assurance that it can meet its future milestones. We made three recommendations aimed at ensuring that USCIS takes a comprehensive and cost-effective approach to the development and deployment of transformation efforts to meet the agency's goals of improved adjudications and customer services processes. In its comments on our report, DHS reported that USCIS is taking action to address each recommendation.

---

[7]GAO, *Department of Homeland Security: Progress Made and Work Remaining in Implementing Homeland Security Missions 10 Years after 9/11*, GAO-11-881 (Washington, D.C.: Sept. 7, 2011).

[8]GAO, *Immigration Benefits: Consistent Adherence to DHS's Acquisition Policy Could Help Improve Transformation Program Outcomes*, GAO-12-66 (Nov. 22, 2011).

Performance Information Can Be Used to Measure the Federal Government's Progress toward Addressing Issues

After identifying issues, Congress has established expectations for the level of performance to be achieved by federal agencies and programs, and regular reporting on results. As highlighted in our case study on efforts to address the global HIV/AIDS pandemic, setting clear goals—with target levels of performance and timeframes for achieving them—and expectations for periodic progress reports helped Congress sustain attention on improving results over the course of several years.

Case Illustration: Coordinating U.S. Efforts to Address the Global HIV/AIDS Pandemic

In 2003, Congress found that HIV/AIDS had reached pandemic proportions during the previous 20 years, and that by the end of 2002, an estimated 42 million individuals were infected with HIV or living with AIDS.[9] In addition, Congress found that the U.S. government had the capacity to lead and enhance the effectiveness of the international community's response, but it required strong coordination among various agencies to ensure the effective and efficient use of financial and technical resources to provide international HIV/AIDS assistance.[10] However, at that time, the U.S. government funded separate HIV/AIDS foreign assistance programs in several agencies as well as directly to the Global Fund to Fight AIDS, Tuberculosis and Malaria.[11] To address these issues, Congress authorized a 5-year initiative—also known as the President's Emergency Plan for AIDS Relief, or PEPFAR—to establish a comprehensive, integrated 5-year strategy to fight global HIV/AIDS.[12] Congress authorized up to $15 billion in funding and created a streamlined U.S. approach to global HIV/AIDS treatment by coordinating and deploying federal agencies and resources through a single entity: the Office of the U.S. Global AIDS Coordinator (OGAC) within the Department of State.

---

[9]United States Leadership Against HIV/AIDS, Tuberculosis, and Malaria Act of 2003, Pub. L. No. 108-25, § 2(1), (3)(A), 117 Stat. 711, 712 (2003).

[10]Pub. L. No. 108-25, § 2(22), (24).

[11]The Global Fund to Fight AIDS, Tuberculosis and Malaria is a multilateral, non-profit, public-private mechanism to rapidly disburse grants to augment existing spending on the prevention and treatment of HIV/AIDS, tuberculosis, and malaria while maintaining significant oversight of financial transactions and program effectiveness.

[12]Pub. L. No. 108-25, 117 Stat. 711 (2003).

Congress established a performance goal to support treatment for 2 million people infected with HIV/AIDS by 2006.[13] In addition, for the 5-year period covered by the initial authorization, fiscal years 2004 through 2008, PEPFAR sought to prevent 7 million new HIV infections and support care for 10 million people infected and affected by HIV/AIDS. As required in the authorizing legislation, OGAC reported annually to Congress on the progress being made under PEPFAR. This information proved useful to congressional decision makers leading up to reauthorization in 2008. For example, the House Committee on Foreign Affairs held a hearing in April 2007 to assess PEPFAR's progress and challenges in combating the global HIV/AIDS pandemic. During his opening remarks, the committee's chairman provided an update of performance under PEPFAR to date:

"So far we can say that this critically important legislation is working. It has supplied lifesaving antiretroviral therapy to more than 800,000 adults and children, provided invaluable testing and counseling for 19 million, supported essential services to prevent mother-to-child transmission to more than 6 million women and served 4.5 million people with desperately needed care and support. These numbers represent solid progress toward the program's stated 5-year goal of 5 million treated with antiretrovirals, 7 million infections averted and care provided to 10 million patients."[14]

Congress reauthorized PEPFAR and provided up to $48 billion through fiscal year 2013 in the Tom Lantos and Henry J. Hyde United States Global Leadership Against HIV/AIDS, Tuberculosis, and Malaria Reauthorization Act of 2008 (2008 Leadership Act).[15] The 2008 Leadership Act also established new 5-year goals, which among others, include assisting partner countries to

- support the increase in number of individuals receiving antiretroviral treatment above 2 million;
- prevent 12 million new HIV infections worldwide; and

---

[13]Pub. L. No. 108-25, § 402(a)(3).

[14]*PEPFAR: An Assessment of Progress and Challenges, Hearing before the H. Comm. on Foreign Affairs*, 110th Cong. 2 (2007) (statement by Chairman Tom Lantos).

[15]Pub. L. No. 110-293, 122 Stat. 2918 (2008).

- support care for 12 million people infected with or affected by HIV/AIDS, including 5 million orphans and vulnerable children affected by HIV/AIDS.[16]

Since then, Congress has continued to monitor progress towards the updated goals. For example, in September 2010, the House Committee on Foreign Affairs held another hearing assessing PEPFAR's progress and challenges in addressing the global HIV/AIDS pandemic. In addition, we have issued several reports[17] reviewing various aspects of PEPFAR— such as the selection and oversight of organizations implementing PEPFAR activities and global HIV/AIDS program monitoring—in response to directives contained in the 2008 Leadership Act[18] and the Consolidated Appropriations Act of 2008.[19]

Performance Information Can Help Identify Better Strategies to Address Issues

Finally, Members of Congress, congressional committees, and staff can assess whether existing strategies are the most efficient and effective means for agencies to meet their goals. Analyzing existing performance information can help identify new strategies that could lead to improved results. As the case study on addressing improper payments shows, when it is clear that agencies are not meeting performance expectations, Congress has provided agencies with additional authorities and required alternate approaches to achieve results.

Case Illustration: Identifying and Addressing Improper Payments

The federal government is accountable for how its agencies and grantees spend hundreds of billions of taxpayer dollars annually, including safeguarding those expenditures against improper payments and establishing mechanisms to recoup those funds when overpayments

---

[16]Pub. L. No. 110-293, § 101(a).

[17]For example, see GAO, *President's Emergency Plan for AIDS Relief: Program Planning and Reporting*, GAO-11-785 (Washington, D.C.: July 29, 2011), *President's Emergency Plan for AIDS Relief: Efforts to Align Programs with Partner Countries' HIV/AIDS Strategies and Promote Partner Country Ownership*, GAO-10-836 (Washington, D.C.: Sept. 20, 2010), and *President's Emergency Plan for AIDS Relief: Partner Selection and Oversight Follow Accepted Practices but Would Benefit from Enhanced Planning and Accountability*, GAO-09-666 (Washington, D.C.: July 15, 2009).

[18]Pub. L. No. 110-293, § 101(d).

[19]Pub. L. No. 110-161, § 668(d), 121 Stat. 1844, 2353 (2007).

occur.[20] Since fiscal year 2000, we have issued a number of reports and testimonies, at the request of Congress, aimed at raising the level of attention and corrective actions surrounding improper payments. Our work has highlighted long-standing, widespread, and significant problems with improper payments across the federal government. For example, we reported in 2000 that the full extent of improper payments governmentwide remained largely unknown, hampering efforts to reduce such payments since many agencies did not attempt to identify or estimate improper payments while others only did so for certain programs.[21] To help address these issues, Congress passed the Improper Payments Information Act of 2002 (IPIA),[22] which requires executive branch agencies to (1) identify programs and activities susceptible to significant improper payments, (2) estimate the amount of improper payments for those programs and activities, and (3) report these estimates along with actions taken to reduce improper payments for programs with estimates that exceed $10 million.

Congressional oversight helped highlight progress agencies made in identifying and addressing improper payments, but also identified a number of challenges related to IPIA implementation. Six congressional committees and subcommittees held 12 hearings on or related to improper payments from 2004—the first year in which IPIA's reporting requirements were fully implemented—through 2009. Our testimony at an April 2009 hearing before the Senate Committee on Homeland Security and Governmental Affairs Subcommittee on Federal Financial Management, Government Information, Federal Services, and International Security summarized the progress and challenges in

---

[20]We have previously reported that an improper payment is any payment that should not have been made or that was made in an incorrect amount (including overpayments and underpayments) under statutory, contractual, administrative, or other legally applicable requirements. It includes any payment to an ineligible recipient, any payment for an ineligible good or service, any duplicate payment, any payment for a good or service not received (except for such payments where authorized by law), and any payment that does not account for credit for applicable discounts. OMB guidance also instructs agencies to report payments for which insufficient or no documentation was found as improper payments. Accordingly, improper payments do not necessarily represent a loss to the government.

[21]GAO, *Financial Management: Billions in Improper Payments Continue to Require Attention,* GAO-01-44 (Washington, D.C.: Oct. 27, 2000).

[22]Pub. L. No. 107-300, 116 Stat. 2350 (2002).

implementation to date.[23] Although reported improper payment estimates rose substantially from 2004 to 2008, the first 5 fiscal years of IPIA implementation, we reported that this was a positive step in improving transparency over the full magnitude of the federal government's improper payments as more agencies and more programs reported estimates over time (see figure 1). In addition, of the 35 agency programs that reported estimates in each of the 5 fiscal years, 24 of them (or about 69 percent) reported reduced error rates when comparing 2008 rates to those in 2004. However, we identified several major challenges that remained in meeting the goals of IPIA, including that

- the total estimates reported in fiscal year 2008 did not reflect the full scope of improper payments across federal agencies;
- noncompliance issues with IPIA implementation existed; and
- agencies continued to face challenges in the design or implementation of internal controls to identify and prevent improper payments.

We also noted that separate assessments by agency auditors, such as GAO or inspectors general, would help to reliably determine the scope of any deficiencies in, and provide a valuable independent validation of, agencies' efforts to implement IPIA.

---

[23]GAO, *Improper Payments: Progress Made but Challenges Remain in Estimating and Reducing Improper Payments*, GAO-09-628T (Washington, D.C.: Apr. 22, 2009).

Figure 1: Governmentwide Improper Payment Estimates, Fiscal Years 2002 to 2011

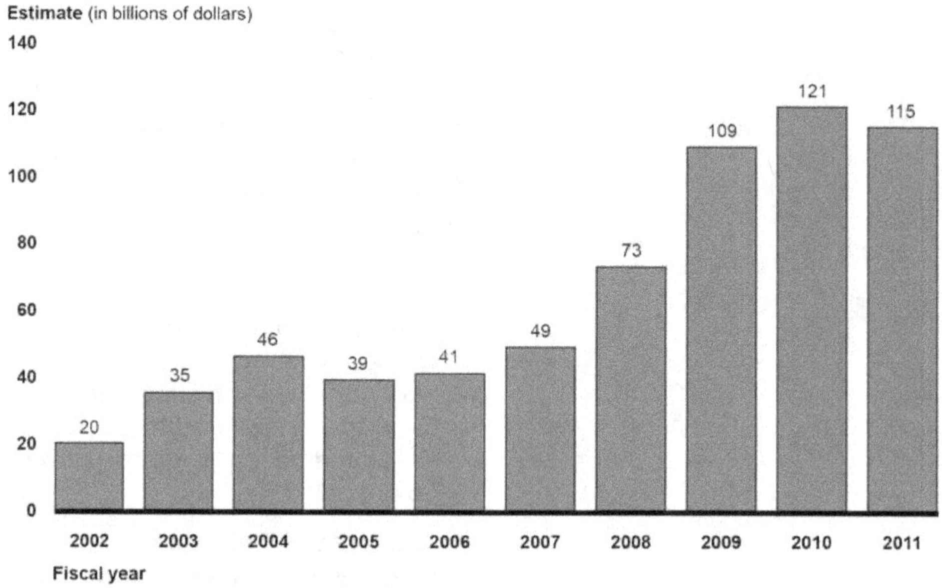

Estimate (in billions of dollars)

Fiscal year	Estimate
2002	20
2003	35
2004	46
2005	39
2006	41
2007	49
2008	73
2009	109
2010	121
2011	115

Source: Annual Financial Report of the United States Government for fiscal years 2002 through 2011.

Note: Improper payment estimates reported by OMB are subject to change over time as agencies update the underlying data. Amounts shown in the chart for 2004–2010 include updated estimates as reported in the Financial Report of the United States Government for the following fiscal year.

To help address these challenges, Congress expanded IPIA's requirements for identifying, estimating, and reporting on programs and activities susceptible to significant improper payments through the Improper Payments Elimination and Recovery Act of 2010 (IPERA).[24] Among other things, IPERA requires (1) agencies to report on their remediation actions and include a summary of the steps they have taken to hold agency officials accountable for meeting improper payment reduction targets and establishing controls, and (2) agency inspectors general to annually determine and report on whether their respective agencies are in compliance with key IPERA requirements. IPERA also included a new, broader requirement for agencies to conduct recovery audits, where cost effective, for each program and activity with at least $1

---

[24]Pub. L. No. 111-204, 124 Stat. 2224 (2010).

million in annual program outlays.[25] In the first year of IPERA
implementation, fiscal year 2011, 17 agencies reported an estimated
$115 billion in improper payments for 79 programs—a decrease of about
$5 billion from revised fiscal year 2010 estimates.[26] In addition, OMB
reported that agencies recaptured about $1.25 billion in improper
payments to contractors, vendors, and health care providers in fiscal year
2011. As we recently reported, OMB also identified improper payments as
an area covered by one of 14 interim crosscutting priority goals in the
President's Budget for fiscal year 2013.[27] The particular goal is to reduce
the governmentwide improper payment rate by at least 2 percentage
points by fiscal year 2014, from 5.42 percent in 2009, and applies to all
federal programs that annually report improper payment estimates.

---

[25]This IPERA provision significantly lowered the threshold for required recovery audits
from $500 million to $1 million and expanded the scope for recovery audits to all programs
and activities.

[26]The reported decrease was primarily related to three programs—decreases in program
outlays for the Department of Labor's Unemployment Insurance program, and decreases
in reported error rates for the Department of the Treasury's Earned Income Tax Credit
program and the Department of Health and Human Services's Medicare Advantage
program.

[27]GAO, *Managing for Results: GAO's Work Related to the Interim Crosscutting Priority
Goals under the GPRA Modernization Act*, GAO-12-620R (Washington, D.C.: May 31,
2012).

Appendix I: Illustrative Questions to Assist Congress in Focusing Consultations on Key Issues

We have previously reported that consultations provide an opportunity for Congress to influence

1. what results agencies should seek to achieve (long-term and annual goals);
2. how those results will be achieved, including how an agency's efforts are aligned and coordinated with other related efforts (strategies and resources);
3. how to measure progress given the complexity of federal programs and activities (performance measures); and
4. how to report on results (reporting).[1]

Table 2 presents examples of questions that Members of Congress and their staffs can ask on strategic plans and related performance issues—during consultations with agencies or in other venues such as hearings—to help ensure that the associated performance information meets their needs and expectations.

---

[1]GAO-12-215R.

Table 2: Illustrative Consultation Questions

Topic 1: Long-term and Annual Goals

1.1.	Are the agency's goals and priorities consistent with those of Congress? If not, why do differences exist and can they be resolved?
1.2.	Do the long-term goals cover the major functions and activities of the agency?
1.3.	Are the long-term goals expressed in a manner that will allow the agency and Congress to assess whether the goals are achieved? If not, is the relationship between the long-term goals and annual goals clearly articulated to allow for progress to be gauged?
1.4.	Are the agency's goals adequately aligned with other federal efforts, such as the agency's contribution to any crosscutting goals or related efforts at other agencies?

Topic 2: Strategies and Resources

2.1.	Are the agency's long-term and annual goals realistic given current and expected resources?
2.2.	Are strategies clearly linked to agency's goals? Are the outlined strategies the most effective and efficient approaches?
2.3.	Does the agency identify the various federal organizations, programs, and activities—within and external to the agency—that contribute to its goals? Are there additional federal entities and efforts that should be included?
2.4.	Does the plan reflect coordination or strategies for working with other agencies as appropriate? If so, how are the agencies working together to ensure that related efforts are complementary appropriate in scope and not unnecessarily duplicative?

Topic 3: Measuring Performance

3.1.	How does or will the agency measure progress toward its goals? In measuring progress, does the agency measure various aspects of its performance—such as cost, customer satisfaction, efficiency, outputs, outcomes, quality, and timeliness—to provide balance among competing demands?
3.2.	Has the agency been meeting established performance targets? If not, are the targets realistic and what actions are being taken to meet future targets?
3.3.	Does the agency provide sufficient information on the validity and accuracy of its performance measures and data to ensure that reported results will be useful for congressional decision making? Would additional information or actions improve its usefulness?

Topic 4: Reporting Results

4.1.	What steps does the agency take to ensure that congressional decision makers are aware that performance results are available?
4.2.	Does the timing and format of the agency's performance reporting align with congressional needs?
4.3.	Would it be useful for interested parties in Congress to receive any of the agency's performance data more frequently or in different formats than the agency is currently reporting them?

Source: GAO.

Appendix II: GAO Contact and Staff Acknowledgments

GAO Contact	J. Christopher Mihm, (202) 512-6806 or mihmj@gao.gov
Staff Acknowledgments	In addition to the above contact, Elizabeth Curda, Assistant Director; Benjamin T. Licht; and Megan M. Taylor made significant contributions to this guide. Todd M. Anderson, Kathryn Bernet, Carla Brown, Gerard Burke, Virginia A. Chanley, Beryl H. Davis, Rebecca Gambler, David Gootnick, Nancy Kingsbury, Susan Offutt, James Michels, Stephanie Shipman, Katherine Siggerud, Bernice Steinhardt, Andrew J. Stephens, Jack Warner, and Dan Webb also made key contributions.

Related GAO Products

Managing for Results: Opportunities for Congress to Address Government Performance Issues. GAO-12-215R. Washington, D.C.: December 9, 2011.

Managing for Results: GPRA Modernization Act Implementation Provides Important Opportunities to Address Government Challenges. GAO-11-617T. Washington, D.C.: May 10, 2011.

Government Performance: GPRA Modernization Act Provides Opportunities to Help Address Fiscal, Performance, and Management Challenges. GAO-11-466T. Washington, D.C.: March 16, 2011.

Government Performance: Strategies for Building a Results-Oriented and Collaborative Culture in the Federal Government. GAO-09-1011T. Washington, D.C.: September 24, 2009.

Government Performance: Lessons Learned for the Next Administration on Using Performance Information to Improve Results. GAO-08-1026T. Washington, D.C.: July 24, 2008.

Congressional Oversight: FAA Case Study Shows How Agency Performance, Budgeting, and Financial Information Could Enhance Oversight. GAO-06-378. Washington, D.C.: March 8, 2006.

Performance Budgeting: PART Focuses Attention on Program Performance, but More Can Be Done to Engage Congress. GAO-06-28. Washington, D.C.: October 28, 2005.

Managing for Results: Enhancing Agency Use of Performance Information for Management Decision Making, GAO-05-927. Washington, D.C.: September 9, 2005.

Results-Oriented Government: GPRA Has Established a Solid Foundation for Achieving Greater Results. GAO-04-38. Washington, D.C.: March 10, 2004.

Managing for Results: Views on Ensuring the Usefulness of Agency Performance Information to Congress. GAO/GGD-00-35. Washington, D.C.: January 26, 2000.

Managing for Results: Enhancing the Usefulness of GPRA Consultations Between the Executive Branch and Congress. GAO/T-GGD-97-56. Washington, D.C.: March 10, 1997.

Managing for Results: Using GPRA to Assist Congressional and Executive Branch Decisionmaking. GAO/T-GGD-97-43. Washington, D.C.: February 12, 1997.

Managing for Results: Achieving GPRA's Objectives Requires Strong Congressional Role. GAO/T-GGD-96-79. Washington, D.C.: March 6, 1996.

Program Evaluation: Improving the Flow of Information to the Congress. GAO/PEMD-95-1. Washington, D.C.: January 30, 1995.

GAO's Mission	The Government Accountability Office, the audit, evaluation, and investigative arm of Congress, exists to support Congress in meeting its constitutional responsibilities and to help improve the performance and accountability of the federal government for the American people. GAO examines the use of public funds; evaluates federal programs and policies; and provides analyses, recommendations, and other assistance to help Congress make informed oversight, policy, and funding decisions. GAO's commitment to good government is reflected in its core values of accountability, integrity, and reliability.
Obtaining Copies of GAO Reports and Testimony	The fastest and easiest way to obtain copies of GAO documents at no cost is through GAO's website (www.gao.gov). Each weekday afternoon, GAO posts on its website newly released reports, testimony, and correspondence. To have GAO e-mail you a list of newly posted products, go to www.gao.gov and select "E-mail Updates."
Order by Phone	The price of each GAO publication reflects GAO's actual cost of production and distribution and depends on the number of pages in the publication and whether the publication is printed in color or black and white. Pricing and ordering information is posted on GAO's website, http://www.gao.gov/ordering.htm. Place orders by calling (202) 512-6000, toll free (866) 801-7077, or TDD (202) 512-2537. Orders may be paid for using American Express, Discover Card, MasterCard, Visa, check, or money order. Call for additional information.
Connect with GAO	Connect with GAO on Facebook, Flickr, Twitter, and YouTube. Subscribe to our RSS Feeds or E-mail Updates. Listen to our Podcasts. Visit GAO on the web at www.gao.gov.
To Report Fraud, Waste, and Abuse in Federal Programs	Contact: Website: www.gao.gov/fraudnet/fraudnet.htm E-mail: fraudnet@gao.gov Automated answering system: (800) 424-5454 or (202) 512-7470
Congressional Relations	Katherine Siggerud, Managing Director, siggerudk@gao.gov, (202) 512-4400, U.S. Government Accountability Office, 441 G Street NW, Room 7125, Washington, DC 20548
Public Affairs	Chuck Young, Managing Director, youngc1@gao.gov, (202) 512-4800 U.S. Government Accountability Office, 441 G Street NW, Room 7149 Washington, DC 20548